Carleton's Mo
Saves the Grotto

Written by Helen Yoxall Burns

Illustrated by Jared Burki

For Pippa and Claudia—H.Y.B.

For my two sons Zayn and Yusuf—J.B.

‘Twas the week before Christmas when at Carleton House,
Not a creature was stirring, except for a mouse.
Such a miniature mouse, dressed in tiny grey clothes,
With a long hairless tail and a pointed pink nose.

Carleton Mouse was his name, Carleton House was his home,
And long after home-time, dear Carleton would roam.
When the teachers were nestled all snug in their beds,
While visions of super sums danced in their heads.

In and out of the classrooms from his mini mousehole,
Carleton scampered and scurried on playground patrol.
But one cold, dark night, as he watched the Head leave,
Mrs Coleman spoke softly to Caretaker Steve.

"All our children have worked so incredibly hard,
But the blizzard has covered the whole of the yard.
Santa's coming tomorrow but so is more snow,
How will poor Santa know which way to go?"

"A big blizzard is brewing! The air is so brisk!
What if school freezes? The grotto's at risk!"
Carleton couldn't believe his big, rounded ears,
So he scurried and scuttled to share his big fears.

But, of course, Stanley Sloth was asleep in a chair,
Daisy Duck tucked up with Freddy the Bear.
Max, the Maths Monkey, was off counting sheep,
Carleton Mouse puffed his chest:

"PLEASE WAKE UP FROM YOUR SLEEP!"

A B C
Y Z

Only Lola and Monty awoke from the noise.

"*Listen up,*" explained Carleton. "*Our girls and our boys,*

Will be saddened if bad snow stops Santa tonight...."

But mean Monty was cruel about Carleton's height.

"I am not being rude, but hey, dude—you're too small!

You can't fight Mother Nature when snow starts to fall.

Are you after a Merit or Star of the Week?!

Go to bed, Carleton, before the weather turns bleak."

With his long hairless tail tucked between little legs,
Carleton scampered and scurried along the coat pegs.
"If 'They Can Because They Think They Can'—I CAN TOO!
But I'm in a pickle." What could Carleton do?

So he turned up his collar and pulled down his cap,
"I must settle my brain for a long winter's nap."
But as Carleton drew near to the green reading pod,
He saw something was different; something was odd.

THEY CAN BECAUSE THEY THINK THEY CAN
CARLETON HOUSE

From the light of the moon, through the pod's door ajar,
White snow-buried shapes, *"Mr Witter's guitar!"*
Carleton's bed was now under a blanket of snow,
He had nowhere to sleep! Where on earth could he go?

Through the prayer garden, playground and into the Hall,
Carleton raced at a pace but he slipped off the wall.
His landing was soft into blue, grey and white,
The lost property box, to cold Carleton's delight!

It was full of lost items, none with name tags,
Water bottles and cardigans, ties and book bags.
"*Frilly socks, football socks, long socks for bed.
P.E socks, enough socks to...I've got it!*" Carleton said.

He scooped up the socks in his tiny pink paws,
With a vast master plan to attract Santa Claus.
His next stop—the art shelf for anything bright,
And he set up his table to work through the night.

With a scatter of glitter, a garnish of glue,
A splatter of paint, he made one and then two.
Quite soon, forty, then fifty, amounts were untold,
The adorned socks were ready! Now out to the cold!

But his bunting of socks tied together with string,
Was too heavy for him, so a feathery wing
Surprised Carleton Mouse—then a kind, furry paw
Helped pull the creations out of the door.

STICK

With the string in their mouths, the light-footed squad,
Tied one end of string to the white reading pod.
On the other end, Carleton and Daisy took flight,
To the bus stop, the post box, the red traffic light.

Once back in the yard there arose such a noise,
They sprang up to see a big sleigh full of toys.

"Now, Dasher! Now, Dancer!
Now Prancer and Vixen!
On, Comet! On, Cupid!
On, Donner and Blitzen!"

Santa's sleigh screeched and skidded. "*Here, girls, we must stop!*
There's one hundred and eighty-odd presents to drop!"
As one hundred and eighty-odd socks filled up high,
Santa called to his reindeer to head to the sky.

"*To the top of the porch, to the top of the house,*
We all owe our thanks to that little white mouse!"
Carleton waved Santa off as he drove out of sight,
"*Happy Christmas to all, and to all, a good night!*"

About the Author

Helen Yoxall Burns has been writing in rhyme for a very long time (see)! For over twenty years, she has written fun, personal poetry to make Big People Smile at special occasions. In 2020, Helen decided to follow her dream of making Little People Smile as well, so set on a magical quest to learn everything she could about writing children's picture books.

Inspired by reading nightly with her two Pink Bookworms, Helen loves reading and writing special stories sprinkled with a magical message. She also loves long walks in her local park, planning special events and spending time with her extended family.

Oh My Words

@oh_my_words_

oh_my_words_

About the Illustrator

Jared Burki is a medical doctor, artist and illustrator. As a child, his scientific curiosity inspired him to sketch human anatomy, like a 'little Leonardo'. His fascination with how the body works led him to a career in medicine. Undoubtedly, his creative spark is encouraged by his wonderful wife, the antics of his two beautiful boys and Persian cats. "As a doctor, I am blessed to be able to assist people in their times of need. With my art, I hope to inspire young minds as they explore and experience worlds of wonder."

Acknowledgements

A huge thank you to author Jude Lennon for her ongoing encouragement. Her creative writing course in 2020 propelled me into the creative writing world, for which I am very grateful!

Jude also introduced me to TAUK Publishing, to whom I owe a very special thank you. Their expertise, guidance, and impressive tight-deadline skills(!) have created a dream come true. Thank you to Estelle Maher and Sue Miller at TAUK and designer Sarah Fountain for making this book a reality.

Thank you to my best friend and shining star, Charlotte, whose vast literary knowledge and support for her friend's dreams were in equal measure. Love and miss you, always.

Huge thanks and praise to Jared Burki for his outstanding illustrations. I'm forever grateful that our chat at the school gates many years ago led us to this exciting path!

A big thank you to my unsuspecting BETA readers, my husband JB, and my mum and dad Ellen and John. The family group chat can rest now!

Thank you to my critique group at Write Mentor and author Clare Helen Welsh for their invaluable feedback.

With Very Special Thanks To

Carleton House Preparatory School for allowing me to bring their magnificent mascot to life. *"They Can Because They Think They Can."*

Printed in Great Britain
by Amazon